# Contents

144174

# Use of Guidance

## THE APPROVED DOCUMENTS

The Building Regulations 1991, which come into operation on 1 June 1992, replace the Building Regulations 1985 (SI 1985 No. 1065) and consolidate all subsequent revisions to those regulations. This document is one of a series that has been approved by the Secretary of State as practical guidance on meeting the requirements of Schedule 1 and regulation 7 of the Building Regulations.

**At the back of this document is a list of those documents currently published by the Department of the Environment and the Welsh Office which have been approved for the purpose of the Building Regulations 1991.**

The detailed provisions contained in the Approved Documents are intended to provide guidance for some of the more common building situations. In other circumstances, alternative ways of demonstrating compliance with the requirements may be appropriate.

### Evidence supporting compliance

**There is no obligation to adopt any particular solution contained in an Approved Document if you prefer to meet the relevant requirement in some other way.** However, should a contravention of a requirement be alleged then, if you have followed the guidance in the relevant Approved Documents, that will be evidence tending to show that you have complied with the Regulations. If you have not followed the guidance then that will be evidence tending to show that you have not complied. It will then be for you to demonstrate by other means that you have satisfied the requirement.

### Other requirements

The guidance contained in an Approved Document relates only to the particular requirements of the Regulations which that document addresses. The building work will also have to comply with the requirements of any other relevant paragraphs in Schedule 1 to the Regulations. There are Approved Documents which give guidance on each of the other requirements in Schedule 1 and on regulation 7.

## LIMITATION ON REQUIREMENTS

In accordance with regulation 8, the requirements in Parts A to K and N of Schedule 1 to the Building Regulations do not require anything to be done except for the purpose of securing reasonable standards of health and safety for persons in or about the building.

## MATERIALS AND WORKMANSHIP

Any building work which is subject to requirements imposed by Schedule 1 of the Building Regulations should, in accordance with regulation 7, be carried out with proper materials and in a workmanlike manner.

You may show that you have complied with regulation 7 in a number of ways, for example, by the appropriate use of a product bearing an EC mark in accordance with the Construction Products Directive (89/106/EEC), or by following an appropriate technical specification (as defined in that Directive), a British Standard, a British Board of Agrément Certificate, or an alternative national technical specification of any member state of the European Community which, in use, is equivalent. You will find further guidance in the Approved Document supporting regulation 7 on materials and workmanship.

### Technical specifications

Building Regulations are made for specific purposes; health and safety, energy conservation and the welfare and convenience of disabled people. Standards and technical approvals are relevant guidance to the extent that they relate to these considerations. However, they may also address other aspects of performance such as serviceability or aspects which although they relate to health and safety are not covered by the Regulations.

When an approved document makes reference to a named standard, the relevant version of the standard is the one listed at the end of the publication. However, if this version of the standard has been revised or updated by the issuing standards body, the new version may be used as a source of guidance provided it continues to address the relevant requirements of the Regulations.

The Secretary of State has agreed with the British Board of Agrément on the aspects of performance which it needs to assess in preparing its Certificates in order that the Board may demonstrate the compliance of a product or system which has an Agrément Certificate with the requirements of the Regulations. An Agrément Certificate issued by the Board under these arrangements will give assurance that the product or system to which the Certificate relates, if properly used in accordance with the terms of the Certificate, will meet the relevant requirements.

Similarly, the appropriate use of a product which complies with a European Technical Approval as defined in the Construction Products Directive will also meet the relevant requirements.

# The Requirements

This Approved Document, which takes effect on 1 June 1992, deals with the following requirements from Part C of Schedule 1 to the Building Regulations 1991.

| Requirement | Limits on application |
| --- | --- |
| **Preparation of site**<br>**C1.** The ground to be covered by the building shall be reasonably free from vegetable matter.<br><br>**Dangerous and offensive substances**<br>**C2.** Precautions shall be taken to avoid danger to health and safety caused by substances found on or in the ground to be covered by the building.<br><br>**Subsoil drainage**<br>**C3.** Subsoil drainage shall be provided if it is needed to avoid –<br>(a) the passage of ground moisture to the interior of the building;<br>(b) damage to the fabric of the building.<br><br>**Resistance to weather and ground moisture**<br>**C4.** The walls, floors and roof of the building shall resist the passage of moisture to the inside of the building. | |

# C
# Guidance

## Performance

### C1,2 & 3

In the Secretary of State's view the requirements of C1 C2 & C3 will be met by taking precautions to reduce risks to the health and safety of persons in buildings by safeguarding them and the buildings against the adverse effects of:

a.   vegetable matter, and

b.   contaminants on or in the ground to be covered by the building, and

c.   ground water.

### C4

In the Secretary of State's view the requirement of C4 will be met by:

a.   a floor next to the ground preventing undue moisture from reaching the upper surface of the floor (see Diagram 1);

b.   a wall preventing undue moisture from the ground reaching the inside of the building, and, if it is an outside wall, adequately resisting the penetration of rain and snow to the inside of the building (see Diagram 2);

c.   a roof resisting the penetration of moisture from rain or snow to the inside of the building (see Diagram 3);

d.   ensuring that floors next to the ground, walls and roof are not damaged by moisture from the ground, rain or snow and do not carry that moisture to any part of the building which it would damage.

Damage can be avoided either by preventing moisture from getting to materials which would be damaged or by using materials which will not be damaged.

This document does not give guidance on preventing damage resulting from the condensation of water vapour on cold surfaces. Approved Documents L, Conservation of fuel and power and F, Ventilation should be referred to and also the BRE publication *Thermal insulation: avoiding risks.*

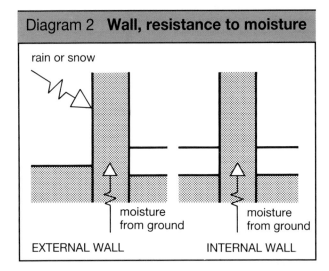

Diagram 1   **Floor, resistance to moisture**

SOLID FLOOR          SUSPENDED FLOOR

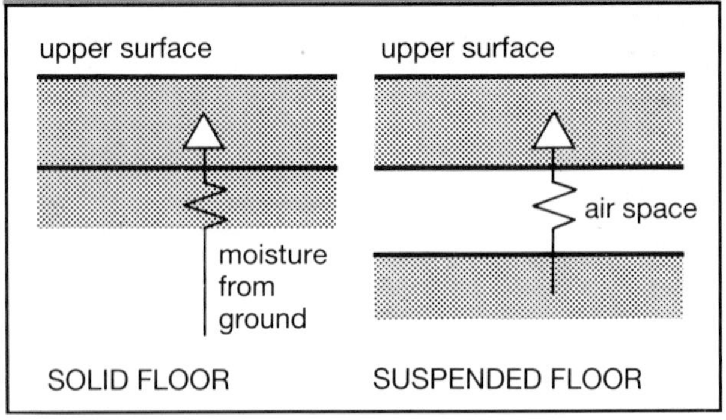

Diagram 2   **Wall, resistance to moisture**

EXTERNAL WALL          INTERNAL WALL

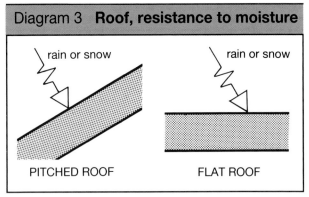

Diagram 3   **Roof, resistance to moisture**

PITCHED ROOF          FLAT ROOF

# Introduction

**0.1** Section 1 of this document deals with site preparation and site drainage. Section 2 deals with contaminants.

**0.2** Section 3 deals with floors next to the ground; Section 4 deals with walls; Section 5 deals with cladding for external walls and roofs.

**0.3** There are several references in this document to moisture damage. The damage in question is damage so serious that it would produce deterioration in a material or structure to the point that it would present an imminent danger to health or safety or (if it is an insulating material) its performance would be permanently reduced.

### Definitions

**0.4** The following meanings apply to terms throughout this Approved Document:

**Floor** Lower surface of any space in a building including finishes that are laid as part of the permanent construction.

**Wall** Vertical construction that includes piers, columns and parapets. It also includes chimneys if they are attached to the building. It does not include windows, doors or similar openings.

**Moisture** Water in the form of a vapour as well as a liquid.

**Contaminant** Any material in or on the ground to be covered by the building (including fæcal or animal matter) and any substance which is, or could become: toxic, corrosive, explosive, flammable or radioactive and so likely to be a danger to health and safety.

# Section 1

## SITE PREPARATION AND SITE DRAINAGE

### Normal site preparation

**1.1**  A building will meet the performance if provisions are made at least to the extent described in this Section.

### Organic material

**1.2**  Turf and other vegetable matter should be removed from the ground to be covered by the building at least to a depth sufficient to prevent later growth.

This provision does not apply to a building which is to be used wholly for:

a.  storing goods, provided that any persons who are habitually employed in the building are engaged only in taking in, caring for, or taking out the goods, or

b.  a purpose such that the provision would not serve to increase protection to the health or safety of any persons habitually employed in the building.

**1.3**  Building services such as below-ground drainage should be sufficiently robust or flexible to accommodate the presence of any roots. Joints should be made so that roots will not penetrate them.

### Site drainage

**1.4**  The provisions which follow assume that the site of the building is not subject to flooding or, if it is, that appropriate steps are being taken.

**1.5**  Where the water table can rise to within 0.25 m of the lowest floor of the building, or where surface water could enter or adversely affect the building either the ground to be covered by the building should be drained by gravity or other effective means of safeguarding the building should be taken. (see Alternative Approach para 1.7)

**1.6**  If an active subsoil drain is cut during excavation it should:

a.  if it is to pass through the building be re-laid in pipes with sealed joints and have access points outside the building, or

b.  be re-routed around the building, or

c.  be re-run to another outfall. (see Diagram 1)

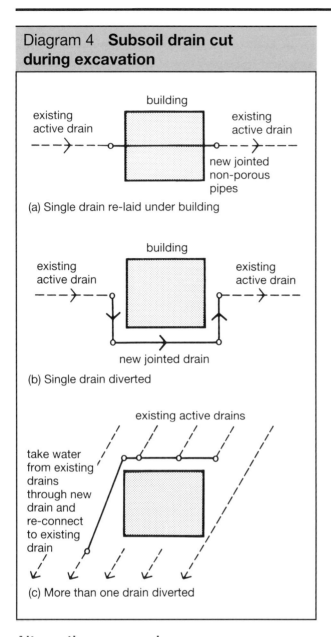

## Diagram 4  Subsoil drain cut during excavation

building

existing active drain

existing active drain

new jointed non-porous pipes

(a) Single drain re-laid under building

building

existing active drain

existing active drain

new jointed drain

(b) Single drain diverted

existing active drains

take water from existing drains through new drain and re-connect to existing drain

(c) More than one drain diverted

## Alternative approach

**1.7** The performance will be met if, as an alternative to providing or re-routing subsoil drainage, the building is designed and constructed to prevent the passage of ground and surface water to the inside or to materials which would be adversely affected by it. (see Sections 3 - 5 Resistance to weather and ground moisture).

## CONTAMINANTS

**2.1** In addition to solid and liquid contaminants arising out of a previous use of land, problems can arise due to gases (see paragraph 0.4 for the meaning of contaminant).

Natural contamination by the radioactive gas radon and its decay products can be a problem in certain parts of the country (see paragraph 2.7).

The burial of waste in landfills can give rise to substantial quantities of landfill gas (see paragraph 2.8).

### Signs of contaminants

**2.2** Sites where the ground to be covered by the building is likely to contain contaminants may be identified at an early stage from planning records or from local knowledge of previous uses. Examples of such sites are given in Table 1. However, there may be occasions when a site has not been identified and the presence of contaminants is only suspected later. Some signs of the possible presence of contaminants are given in Table 2.

Note that the ground to be covered by a building includes the ground to be covered by its foundations.

### Table 1  Sites likely to contain contaminants

Asbestos works
Chemical works
Gas works, coal carbonisation plants and ancillary byproduct works
Industries making or using wood preservatives
Landfill and other waste disposal sites
Metal mines, smelters, foundries, steel works and metal finishing works
Munitions production and testing sites
Nuclear installations
Oil storage and distribution sites
Paper and printing works
Railway land, especially the larger sidings and depots
Scrap yards
Sewage works, sewage farms and sludge disposal sites
Tanneries

**2.3** If any signs of possible contaminants are present the Environmental Health Officer should be told at once. If he confirms the presence of any of the contaminants listed in Table 2 the relevant actions described will meet the performance. These actions assume that the ground to be covered by the building will have at least 100mm of insitu concrete laid over it. See also Alternative approach, paragraphs 2.5 and 2.6.

### Table 2  Possible contaminants and actions

| Signs of possible contaminants | Possible contaminant | Relevant Action |
|---|---|---|
| Vegetation (absence, poor or unnatural growth) | Metals<br>Metal compounds* | None |
| | Organic compounds<br>Gases | Removal |
| Surface materials (unusual colours and contours may indicate wastes and residues) | Metals<br>Metal compounds* | None |
| | Oily and tarry wastes | Removal, filling or sealing |
| | Asbestos (loose) | Filling or sealing |
| | Other mineral fibres | None |
| | Organic compounds including phenols | Removal or filling |
| | Combustible material including coal and coke dust | Removal or filling |
| | Refuse and waste | Total removal or see guidance |
| Fumes and odours (may indicate organic chemicals at very low concentrations) | Flammable explosive and asphyxiating gases including methane and carbon dioxide | Removal |
| | Corrosive liquids | Removal, filling or sealing |
| | Fæcal animal and vegetable matter (biologically active) | Removal or filling |
| Drums and Containers (whether full or empty) | Various | Removal with all contaminated ground |

Note  Liquid and gaseous contaminants are mobile and the ground covered by the building can be affected by such contaminants from elsewhere. Some guidance on landfill gas and radon is given in this document; other liquids and gases should be referred to a specialist.
* Special cement may be needed with sulphates.

**2.4** Terms used in Table 2 have the following meanings:

**Removal** means that the contaminant itself and any contaminated ground to be covered by the building should be taken out to a depth of 1m (or less if the local authority or approved inspector agrees) below the level of the lowest floor and taken away.

**Filling** means that the ground to be covered by the building is to be covered to a depth of 1m (or less if the local authority or approved inspector agrees) with a material which will not react adversely with any contaminant remaining and will be suitable for making up levels. The type of filling and the design of the ground floor should be considered together. Combustible material should be adequately compacted to avoid combustion.

**Sealing** means that a suitable imperforate barrier is laid between the contaminant and the building and sealed at the joints, around the edges and at the service entries. Note that polyethylene may not be suitable if the contaminant is a liquid such as a tarry waste or organic solvent.

## Alternative approach

**2.5** In the most hazardous conditions only the total removal of contaminants from the ground to be covered by the building can provide a complete remedy. In other cases remedial measures can reduce the risks to acceptable levels. These measures should only be undertaken with the benefit of expert advice.

Where the actions described would, for example, involve the removal and handling of large quantities of material, remedial measures which will achieve compliance with the regulations may be possible, but they should only be undertaken with the benefit of expert advice.

**2.6** The BS Draft for Development DD 175:1988 *Code of practice for the identification of potentially contaminated land and its investigation* gives guidance on site investigation and further information on sites in general is given in BS 5930:1981 *Code of practice for site investigations.*

# Gaseous contaminants

## Radon
**2.7** Radon is a naturally-occurring, radioactive, colourless and odourless gas which is formed in small quantities by radioactive decay wherever uranium and radium are found. It can move through the subsoil and so into buildings. Some parts of the country, notably the West Country, have higher natural levels than elsewhere. Exposure to high levels for long periods increases the risk of developing lung cancer. Where a house or extension is to be erected in Cornwall or Devon or parts of Somerset, Northamptonshire or Derbyshire there may be radon contamination of the site and precautions against radon may be necessary.

Guidance on the construction of dwellings in areas susceptible to radon has been published by the Building Research Establishment as a Report.

The precise areas where measures should be taken are reviewed by the Department of the Environment in the light of advice from the National Radiological Protection Board as this becomes available, and are listed in the BRE guidance document, *Radon: guidance on protective measures for new dwellings* updated as necessary. Current information on the areas delimited by the Department of the Environment for the purpose of Building Regulations can be obtained from local authority building control officers or from approved inspectors.

## Landfill gas and methane
**2.8** Landfill gas is generated by the action of anaerobic micro-organisms on biodegradable material and generally consists of methane and carbon dioxide with small quantities of other gases. It can migrate under pressure through the subsoil and through cracks and fissures into buildings.

Gases similar to landfill gas can also arise naturally and should be treated in the same way as those arising from landfills.

Methane is an asphyxiant, will burn, and can explode in air. Carbon dioxide is non-flammable and toxic. Many of the other components of landfill gas are flammable and some are toxic.

## General approach
**2.9** Where the ground to be covered by a building is on, or within 250 m of, landfill, or where there is reason to suspect that there may be gaseous contamination of the ground or where the building will be within the likely sphere of influence of a landfill where gas production is possible, further investigation should be made to determine what, if any, protective measures are necessary.

**2.10** Guidance on the construction of some buildings near but not on landfill sites has been published by the Building Research Establishment as a Report. For such buildings the BRE guidance can be followed. The broad guidelines for dwellings are:

a. Where the level of methane in the ground is unlikely to exceed 1% by volume and the construction of the ground floor of a house or similar small building is of suspended concrete and ventilated as described in the BRE publication, no further protection needs to be provided.

b. The concentration of carbon dioxide must also be considered and should be judged independently of the methane concentration. A carbon dioxide concentration of greater than $1^1/_2$% by volume in the ground indicates a need to consider possible measures to prevent gas ingress. A 5% by volume level in the ground implies that specific design measures are required.

c. The use of permanent continuous mechanical ventilation to ensure that methane or carbon dioxide does not accumulate at any time in or under a house is not usually feasible since there is no management system to look after it. Passive protection is generally the only viable alternative and is effective only where gas concentrations in the ground are low and likely to remain so.

**2.11** In other cases and for non-domestic buildings, expert advice should be sought. If the expert so advises, there should be a complete investigation into the nature of any hazardous gases and their source and the potential of the landfill site for future gas generation.

The amount of gas in the ground as well as its pressure relative to atmosphere also needs to be considered. A low level of gas due to the presence of a small quantity of material or associated with previous control measures may need no remedial measures. High gas concentrations have less impact if the volume of gas is very small such as from limited deposits of peat, silt etc.

The investigation together with expert advice should be used to assess the present and future risk posed by the gas and should include extended monitoring, if necessary. Design of protective measures should be incorporated into the overall design of the building with the detailed assistance of experts in the field and satisfactory arrangements should be made for maintenance and monitoring.

Information and guidance on the site investigation are given in the documents listed in paragraph 2.12.

## References
**2.12**

a.  Department of Environment (Her Majesty's Inspectorate of Pollution). *The Control of Landfill Gas,* Waste Management Paper No.27 (1989), HMSO.

b.  British Standards Institution Draft for Development: *Code of Practice for the Identification of Potentially Contaminated Land and its Investigation* DD 175: 1988.

c.  Crowhurst, D *"Measurement of gas emissions from contaminated land".* BRE Report 1987. HMSO ISBN 0 85125 246 X.

d.  ICRCL 17/78 *Notes on the development and after-use of landfill sites.* 8th edition December 1990. Interdepartmental Committee on the Redevelopment of Contaminated Land.*

e.  ICRCL 59/83 *Guidance on the assessment and redevelopment of contaminated land.* 2nd edition July 1987. Interdepartmental Committee on the Redevelopment of Contaminated Land.*

f.  Institute of Wastes Management. *Monitoring of Landfill Gas* Sept. 1989.

g.  BS 5930: 1981 *Code of practice for site investigations.*

h.  BRE *Radon: guidance on protective measures for new dwellings.* BRE Report. Garston, BRE, 1991. ISBN 0 85125 511 6

j.  BRE *Construction of new buildings on gas contaminated land.* BRE Report. Garston, BRE, 1991. ISBN 0 85125 513 2

* Obtainable from: Department of Environment Publication Sales Unit, Building 1 Victoria Road, South Ruislip, Middlesex HA4 0NZ.

# Section 3

## FLOORS NEXT TO THE GROUND

**3.1** This Section gives guidance for three types of ground floor:

a. **ground supported floors** (see paragraphs 3.3 to 3.8)

b. **suspended timber floors** (see paragraphs 3.9 to 3.11)

c. **suspended concrete floors** (see paragraphs 3.12 to 3.14).

Refer to paragraph 0.4 for the meaning of floor.

**3.2** A floor next to the ground should:

a. resist ground moisture from reaching the upper surface of the floor (see Diagram 5) This provision does not apply to a building to be used wholly for -

i. storing goods or accommodating plant or machinery, provided that any persons who are habitually employed in the building are engaged only in storing, caring for or removing the goods, plant or machinery, or

ii. a purpose such that the provision would not serve to increase protection to the health or safety of any persons habitually employed in the building, and

b. not be damaged by moisture from the ground.

### Diagram 5  Ground supported floor - principle

See para 3.2

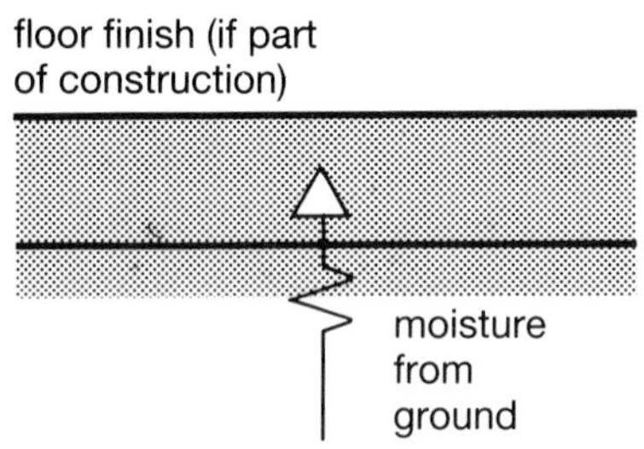

floor finish (if part of construction)

moisture from ground

## Ground supported floors

**3.3** Any ground supported floor will meet the performance if the ground is covered with dense concrete laid on a hardcore bed and a damp-proof membrane is provided. Insulation may be incorporated.

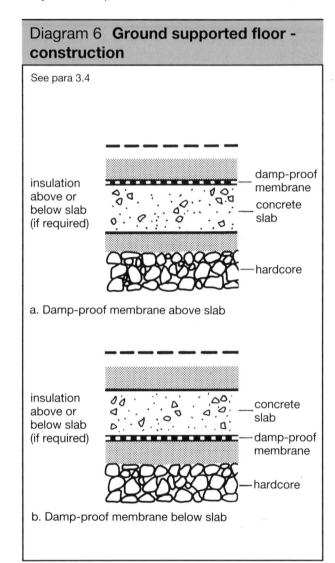

### Diagram 6  Ground supported floor - construction

See para 3.4

insulation above or below slab (if required)

damp-proof membrane

concrete slab

hardcore

a. Damp-proof membrane above slab

insulation above or below slab (if required)

concrete slab

damp-proof membrane

hardcore

b. Damp-proof membrane below slab

---

## Technical solution

**3.4** A concrete ground supported floor may be built as follows (see Diagram 6) (unless it is subjected to water pressure, in which case see Alternative approach, paragraph 3.8):

a.  hardcore bed of clean broken brick or similar inert material, free from materials including water-soluble sulphates in quantities which could damage the concrete, and

b.  concrete at least 100mm thick (but thicker if the structural design requires) and composed of 50kg of cement to not more than $0.11m^3$ of fine aggregate and $0.16m^3$ of coarse aggregate or BS 5328 mix ST2. If there is embedded steel, the concrete should be composed of 50kg of cement to not more than $0.08m^3$ of fine aggregate and $0.13m^3$ of coarse aggregate or BS 5328 mix ST4, and

c.  damp-proof membrane above or below the concrete, and continuous with the damp-proof courses in walls, piers and the like.

**3.5** A membrane laid below the concrete should be at least $300\mu$m (1200 gauge); $250\mu$m (1000 gauge) polythene in accordance with appropriate BBA certificate or to the PIFA standard is also satisfactory.

**3.6** A membrane laid above the concrete should be either polyethylene sheet as described above (but without the bedding material) or three coats of cold applied bitumen solution or similar moisture and water-vapour resisting material. In each case it should be protected either by a screed or a floor finish, unless the membrane is pitchmastic or similar material which will also serve as a floor finish.

**3.7** A timber floor finish laid directly on concrete may be bedded in a material which may also serve as a damp-proof membrane. Timber fillets laid in the concrete as a fixing for a floor finish should be treated with an effective preservative unless they are above the damp-proof membrane. Some preservative treatments are described in BS 1282: 1975 *Guide to the choice, use and application of wood preservatives.*

## Alternative approach

**3.8** The performance (see paragraph 0.4 above) can also be achieved by following the relevant recommendations of Clause 11 of CP 102: 1973 *Protection of buildings against water from the ground.* BS 8102:1990 *Code of practice for protection of structures against water from the ground* includes recommendations for floors subject to water pressure.

# Suspended timber ground floors

**3.9** Any suspended timber floor next to the ground will meet the performance if:

a.  the ground is covered so as to resist moisture and prevent plant growth, and

b.  there is a ventilated air space between the ground covering and the timber, and

c.  there are damp-proof courses between the timber and any material which can carry moisture from the ground (see Diagram 7).

## Diagram 7 Suspended timber floor - principle

See para 3.9

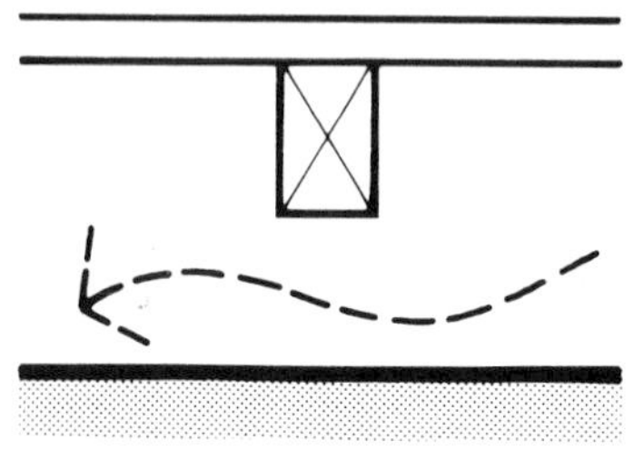

suspended timber floor

ventilated air space

ground cover

## Technical solution

**3.10** A suspended timber floor next to the ground may be built as follows (see Diagram 8), (unless it is covered with a floor finish which is highly vapour resistant, in which case see Alternative approach - paragraph 3.11):

a.  ground covering either-
i.  concrete at least 100mm thick, composed of 50kg of cement to not more than 0.13m³ of fine aggregate and 0.18m³ of coarse aggregate or BS 5328 mix ST I if there is no embedded steel. The concrete should be laid on a hardcore bed of clean broken brick or any other inert material free from materials including water-soluble sulphates in quantities which could damage the concrete, or

ii.  concrete composed as described above or inert fine aggregate, in either case at least 50mm thick laid on at least 300$\mu$m (1200 gauge); 250$\mu$m (1000 gauge) polythene in accordance with appropriate BBA certificate or to the PIFA standard is also satisfactory.

To prevent water collecting on the ground covering, either the top should be entirely above the highest level of the adjoining ground or the covering should be laid to fall to a drainage outlet above the lowest level of the adjoining ground (see Diagram 9).

b.  ventilated air space measuring at least 75mm from the ground covering to the underside of any wall plates and at least 150mm to the underside of the suspended timber floor (or insulation if provided).

Two opposing external walls should have ventilation openings placed so that the ventilating air will have a free path between opposite sides and to all parts. The openings should be large enough to give an actual opening of at least equivalent to 1500mm² for each metre run of wall. Any pipes needed to carry ventilating air should have a diameter of at least 100mm.

c.  damp-proof courses of impervious sheet material, engineering brick or slates in cement mortar or other material which will prevent the passage of moisture.

## Alternative approach

**3.11** The performance (see paragraph 0.3 above) can also be met by following the relevant recommendations of Clause 11 of CP 102: 1973 *Protection of buildings against water from the ground.*

## Diagram 8 **Suspended timber floor - construction**

See para 3.10

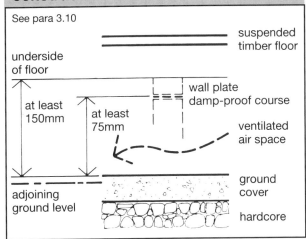

underside of floor

suspended timber floor

at least 150mm

at least 75mm

wall plate
damp-proof course

ventilated air space

adjoining ground level

ground cover

hardcore

## Diagram 9 **Suspended floor - preventing water collection**

See para 3.10a.ii.

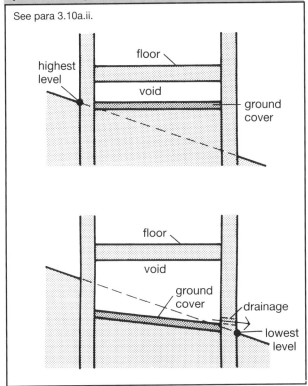

highest level

floor

void

ground cover

floor

void

ground cover

drainage

lowest level

## Diagram 10 **Suspended concrete ground floor**

See para 3.13

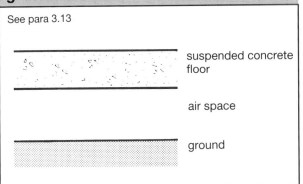

suspended concrete floor

air space

ground

# Suspended concrete ground floors

**3.12** Any suspended floor of in-situ or precast concrete next to the ground will meet the performance if it will adequately resist moisture from reaching the upper surface and if the reinforcement is protected against moisture.

## Technical solution

**3.13** A suspended concrete floor may be built as follows (see Diagram 10):

a. in-situ concrete at least 100mm thick (but thicker if the structural design requires) containing at least 300kg of cement for each $m^3$ of concrete, or

b. precast concrete construction with or without infilling slabs, and

c. reinforcing steel protected by concrete cover of at least 40mm if the concrete is in-situ and at least the thickness required for a moderate exposure if the concrete is precast.

**3.14** A suspended concrete floor should incorporate:

a. damp-proof membrane (to be provided if the ground below the floor has been excavated below the lowest level of the surrounding ground and will not be effectively drained) and

b. in those situations where there is a risk of an accumulation of gas which might lead to an explosion, a ventilated air space. This should measure at least 150mm clear from the ground to the underside of the floor (or insulation if provided).

c. Where the ventilation referred to in b. above is provided two opposing external walls should have ventilation openings placed so that the ventilating air will have a free path between opposite sides and to all parts. The openings should be large enough to give an actual opening of at least equivalent to 1500mm² for each metre run of wall.

Approved Document

**Resistance to weather and ground moisture**

15

# Section 4

## WALLS

**4.1** This Section gives guidance for three situations

a. internal and external walls exposed to moisture from the ground (see paragraphs 4.3 to 4.6)

b. solid external walls exposed to moisture from outside (see paragraphs 4.7 to 4.9), and

c. cavity external walls exposed to moisture from outside (see paragraphs 4.10 to 4.13)

A wall includes piers, columns and parapets. It also includes chimneys if they are attached to the building. A wall does not include windows, doors or similar openings.

**4.2** Walls should:

a. resist the passage of moisture from the ground to the inside of the building (see Diagram 11), and

b. not be damaged by moisture from the ground and not carry moisture from the ground to any part which would be damaged by it

and, if the wall is an external wall:

c. resist the penetration of rain and snow to the inside of the building, and

d. not be damaged by rain and snow and not carry rain and snow to any part which would be damaged by it.

Provisions a and c do not apply to a building to be used wholly for-
i.  storing goods, provided that any persons who are habitually employed in the building are engaged only in storing, caring for or removing the goods, or

ii.  a purpose such that the provision would not serve to increase protection to the health or safety of any persons habitually employed in the building.

### Diagram 11  **Walls - principle**

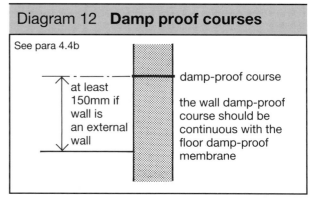

See para 4.2
rain or snow

(a) External wall | moisture from ground | (b) Internal wall | moisture from ground

## Internal and External walls (moisture from the ground)

**4.3** Any internal or external wall will meet the performance if a damp-proof course is provided.

### Technical solution

**4.4** An internal or external wall may be built as follows (unless it is subject to ground water pressure, in which case see Alternative approach - paragraph 4.5):

a. damp-proof course of bituminous material, engineering bricks or slates in cement mortar or any other material that will prevent the passage of moisture. The damp-proof course should be continuous with any damp-proof membrane in the floors, and

b. if the wall is an external wall the damp-proof course should be at least 150mm above the level of the adjoining ground (see Diagram 12) unless the design is such that a part of the building will protect the wall, and

### Diagram 12  **Damp proof courses**

See para 4.4b

at least 150mm if wall is an external wall

damp-proof course

the wall damp-proof course should be continuous with the floor damp-proof membrane

c. if the wall is an external cavity wall the cavity should be taken down at least 150mm below the level of the lowest damp-proof course or a damp-proof tray should be provided so as to prevent rain and snow passing to the inner leaf (see Diagram 13).

### Diagram 13  **Protecting inner leaf**

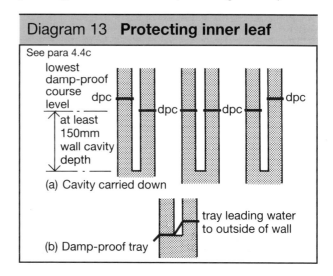

See para 4.4c

lowest damp-proof course level

dpc  dpc  dpc  dpc

at least 150mm wall cavity depth

(a) Cavity carried down

tray leading water to outside of wall

(b) Damp-proof tray

---

## Alternative approach

**4.5** The performance can also be met by following the relevant recommendations of Clauses 4 & 5 of BS8215: 1991 *Code of practice for design and installation of damp-proof courses in masonry construction.* BS 8102: 1990 *Code of practice for protection of structures against water from the ground* includes recommendations for walls subject to ground water pressure including basement walls.

## Additional provisions for external walls (moisture from the outside)

**4.6** As well as giving protection against moisture from the ground an external wall should give protection against rain and snow. This protection can be given by a solid wall of sufficient thickness (see paragraphs 4.7 to 4.9) or by a cavity wall (see paragraphs 4.10 to 4.14) or by an impervious or weather-resisting cladding (see Section 5).

## Solid external walls

**4.7** Any solid wall will meet the performance if it will hold rain and snow until it can be released in a dry period before:

a. penetrating to the inside of the building, or

b. causing damage to the building.

The wall thickness will depend on the type of brick or block and on the severity of the exposure to wind and rain. A method of describing the severity of the exposure to wind-driven rain is described in BSI Draft for Development DD 93: 1984: *Method for assessing exposure to wind-driven rain;* see also BS5628 *Code of practice for use of masonry:* Part 3: 1985 *Materials and components, design and workmanship,* and the BRE publication *Thermal insulation - avoiding risks.*

### Diagram 14 **Solid external wall - severe exposure**

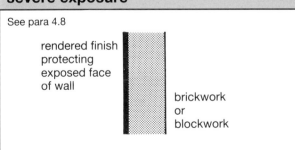

See para 4.8

rendered finish protecting exposed face of wall

brickwork or blockwork

## Technical solution

**4.8** A solid external wall in conditions of **very severe** exposure should be protected by external cladding but in conditions of **severe**

exposure may be built as follows (see Diagram 14):

a. **brickwork** at least 328mm thick, dense aggregate concrete **blockwork** at least 250mm thick, or lightweight aggregate or aerated autoclaved concrete **blockwork** at least 215mm thick, and

b. **rendering:** the exposed face of the bricks or blocks should be rendered or be given no less protection. Rendering should be in two coats with a total thickness of at least 20mm and should have a scraped or textured finish.

The strength of the mortar should be compatible with the strength of the bricks or blocks. The joints, if the wall is to be rendered, should be raked out to a depth of at least 10mm.

The rendering mix should be 1 part of cement, 1 part of lime and 6 parts of well graded sharp sand (nominal mix 1:1:6) unless the blocks are of dense concrete aggregate, in which case the mix may be 1: $^{1}/_{2}$ :4

BS 5262: 1976 *Code of practice. External rendered finishes* includes recommendations for a wider range of mixes according to the severity of the exposure and the type of brick or block.

c. **protection** should be provided where the top of walls etc would otherwise be unprotected (see Diagram 15). Unless the protection and joints will be a complete barrier to moisture, a damp-proof course should also be provided.

### Diagram 15 **Exposed wall - principle**

See para 4.8c

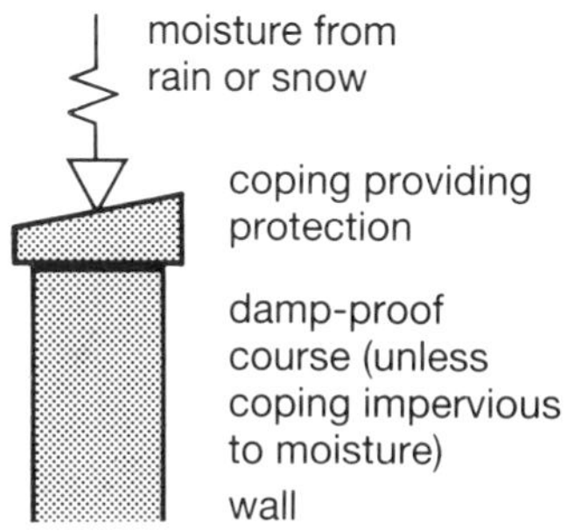

moisture from rain or snow

coping providing protection

damp-proof course (unless coping impervious to moisture)

wall

d. **damp-proof courses** should be provided to direct rain and snow towards the face of the wall as follows (unless the design is such that a part of the building will protect the wall) -

i. where the downward flow will be interrupted by an obstruction, such as a lintel, and

ii. under openings unless there is a sill and the sill and its joints will form a complete barrier, and

iii. where an internal wall is carried up as an external wall.

**4.9** Insulation. A solid external wall may be insulated on the inside or on the outside. Where it is on the inside a cavity should be provided to give a break in the path for moisture and where it is on the outside it should provide some resistance to the ingress of moisture to ensure that the wall remains relatively dry (see Diagram 16 and Section 5).

## Alternative approach

**4.10** The performance can also be met by following the relevant recommendations of:

a. BS 5628 *Code of practice for use of masonry: Part 3: 1985 Materials and components, design and workmanship*. The Code describes alternative constructions to suit the severity of the exposure and the type of brick or block, and

b. BS 5390: 1976 *Code of practice for stone masonry*. Section three of the Code includes recommendations for walls ashlared with stone or cast stone and rubble or rubble faced walls of stone or cast stone.

## Cavity external walls

**4.11** Any external cavity wall will meet the performance if the outer leaf is separated from the inner leaf by a drained air space or in any other way which will prevent rain and snow from being carried to the inner leaf.

## Technical solution

**4.12** A cavity external wall may be built as follows:

a. outer leaf masonry (bricks, blocks, stone or cast stone), and

b. cavity at least 50mm wide. The cavity to be bridged only by wall ties or by damp-proof trays provided to prevent moisture being carried to the inner leaf (see paragraph 4.13 for cavity insulation), and

c. inner leaf masonry or frame with lining.

Where a cavity is to be partially filled, the residual cavity should be not less than 50mm (nominal) wide (see Diagram 16).

## Alternative approach

**4.13** The performance can also be met by following the relevant recommendations of BS 5628 *Code of practice for use of masonry. Part 3: 1985 Materials and components, design and workmanship.* The Code indicates factors affecting rain penetration of cavity walls.

## Cavity insulation

**4.14** An insulating material may be placed in the cavity between the outer leaf and an inner leaf of masonry construction under the following conditions:

a. a rigid thermal insulating material built into the wall should be the subject of a current British Board of Agrément Certificate or a European Technical Approval and the work should be carried out in accordance with the requirements of that document, and

b. urea-formaldehyde foam inserted into the cavity after the wall has been constructed should be in accordance with BS 5617: 1985 *Specification for urea-formaldehyde (UF) foam systems suitable for thermal insulation of cavity walls with masonry or concrete inner and outer leaves* and should be installed in accordance with BS 5618: 1985 *Code of practice for thermal insulation of cavity walls (with masonry or concrete inner and outer leaves) by filling with urea-formaldehyde (UF) foam systems.* The suitability of the wall for foam filling is to be assessed before the work is carried out and the person undertaking the work should hold or operate under a current BSI Certificate of Registration of Assessed Capability or a similar document issued by an equivalent body.

c. other insulating materials inserted into the cavity after the wall has been constructed should be installed in accordance with BS 6232 *Thermal insulation of cavity walls by filling with blown man-made mineral fibre Part 1: 1982 Specification for the performance of installation systems* and Part 2: 1982 *Code of practice for installation of blown man-made mineral fibre in cavity walls with masonry and/ or concrete leaves.* The suitability of the wall for filling is to be assessed before the work is carried out and the person undertaking the work should hold or operate under a current BSI Certificate of Registration of Assessed Capability or a similar document issued by an equivalent body.

Alternatively the insulating material should be the subject of a current British Board of Agrément certificate or a European Technical Approval. The work should be carried out in accordance with the terms of that document by operatives either directly employed by the holder of the document or employed by an installer approved to operate under the document.

**4.15** The suitability of the wall for filling should be assessed before the work is carried out in accordance with BS 8208 *Guide to assessment of suitability of external cavity walls for filling with thermal insulants,* Part 1: 1985 *Existing traditional cavity construction.*

| Diagram 16 **Insulated external walls: examples** |
| --- |

See paras 4.9 and 4.12

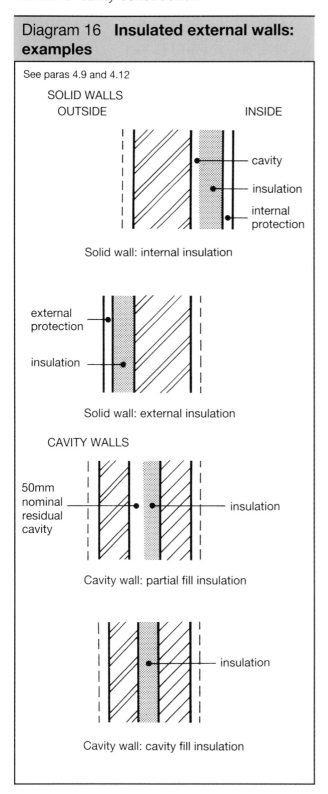

SOLID WALLS

OUTSIDE        INSIDE

cavity

insulation

internal protection

Solid wall: internal insulation

external protection

insulation

Solid wall: external insulation

CAVITY WALLS

50mm nominal residual cavity

insulation

Cavity wall: partial fill insulation

insulation

Cavity wall: cavity fill insulation

# Section 5

## CLADDING FOR EXTERNAL WALLS AND ROOFS

**5.1** Cladding should :

a.  resist the penetration of rain and snow to the inside of the building, and

b.  not be damaged by rain or snow and not carry rain or snow to any part of the building which would be damaged by it. (see Diagram 17)

---

**Diagram 17  Cladding - principle**

See para 5.1

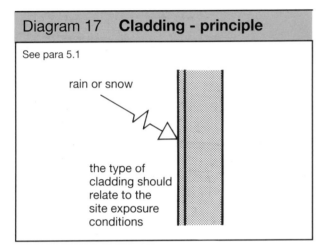

rain or snow

the type of cladding should relate to the site exposure conditions

---

**5.2** Cladding can be designed to protect a building from rain or snow (often driven by the wind) either by holding it at the face of the building or by stopping it from penetrating beyond the back of the cladding. (see Diagram 18)

**5.3** Any cladding will meet the performance if:

a.  it is jointless or has sealed joints, and is impervious to moisture (so that moisture will not enter the cladding), or

b.  it has overlapping dry joints, is impervious or weather-resisting, and is backed by a material which will direct rain or snow which enters the cladding towards the outside face.

**5.4** Some materials can deteriorate rapidly without special care and they should only be used as the weather-resisting part of a wall or roof if certain conditions are met (see Approved Document supporting regulation 7, Materials and workmanship).

The weather-resisting part of a wall or roof does not include paint nor does it include any coating surfacing or rendering which will not itself provide all the weather resistance.

## Technical solution

**5.5**  Cladding may be:

a.  **impervious** including metal, plastic, glass and bituminous products, or

b.  **weather-resisting** including natural stone or slate, cement based products, fired clay and wood, or

c.  **moisture-resisting** including bituminous and plastic products lapped at the joints, if used as a sheet material, and permeable to water vapour unless there is a ventilated space directly behind the material, or

d.  **jointless materials** and **sealed joints,** which should allow for structural and thermal movement.

---

**Diagram 18  Cladding of walls and roofs**

See para 5.2

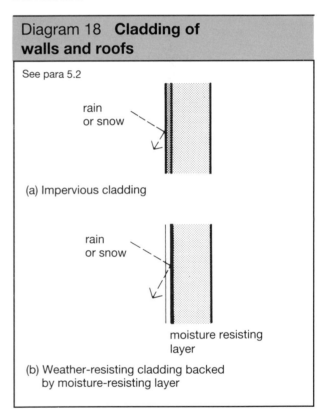

rain or snow

(a) Impervious cladding

rain or snow

moisture resisting layer

(b) Weather-resisting cladding backed by moisture-resisting layer

---

**5.6**  Dry joints between cladding units should be designed so that rain and snow will not pass through them, or the cladding should be designed so that rain or snow which enters the joints will be directed towards the exposed face without it penetrating beyond the back of the cladding.

**Note: Whether dry joints are suitable will depend on the design of the joint or the design of the cladding and the severity of the exposure to wind and rain.**

---

**5.7** Each sheet, tile and section of cladding should be securely fixed.

**5.8** Insulation can be incorporated into the construction provided it is either protected from moisture or is unaffected by it. Problems can arise in such constructions from condensation and from cold bridges; guidance is given in Approved Document F, Ventilation and in the BRE publication *Thermal insulation - avoiding risks.*

## Alternative approach

**5.9** The performance can also be met by following the relevant recommendations of:

a. (for walls and roofs) BS CP 143: *Code of practice for sheet roof and wall coverings.* The Code includes recommendations for:
corrugated and troughed aluminium
(Part 1: 1958),
zinc (Part 5: 1964),
galvanized corrugated steel (Part 10: 1973),
copper (Part 12: 1970 (1988))
aluminium (Part 15: 1973 (1986))
semi-rigid asbestos bitumen sheets (Part 16: 1974),
Recommendations for lead are included in BS6915: 1988 *Specification for design and construction of fully supported lead sheet roof and wall coverings*

b. (for walls and roofs) BS 5247: *Code of practice for sheet wall and floor coverings* Part 14: 1975 *Corrugated asbestos-cement,* and

c. (for walls and steep roofs) BS 8200: 1985 *Code of practice for the design of non load-bearing external vertical enclosures of buildings,* and

d. (for walls only) BS CP 297: 1972 *Precast concrete cladding (non-loadbearing),* and

e. (for walls only) BS 8298: 1989 *Code of practice for design and installation of natural stone cladding and lining.*

These documents describe the materials and contain design considerations including recommendations for fixing.

# C

# Standards referred to

## C1/2/3

BS 5930:1981 *Code of practice for site investigation.*

DD 175:1988 *Code of practice for the identification of potentially contaminated land and its investigation.*

## C4

BS 1282: 1975 *Guide to the choice, use and application of wood preservatives.*

BS 5247 *Code of practice for sheet roof and wall coverings:*
Part 14: 1975 *Corrugated asbestos-cement*
Amendment slips
1: AMD 2821,
2: AMD 3502.

BS 5262: 1976 *Code of practice. External rendered finishes,*
Amendment slips
1: AMD 2103,
2: AMD 6246.

BS 5328: *Concrete:*
Part 1: 1990 *Guide to specifying concrete*
Part 2: 1990 *Method for specifying concrete mixes.*

BS 5390: 1976 (1984) *Code of practice for stone masonry*
Amendment slip
1: AMD 4272.

BS 5617: 1985 *Specification for urea-formaldehyde (UF) foam systems suitable for thermal insulation of cavity walls with masonry or concrete inner and outer leaves.*

BS 5618: 1985 *Code of practice for thermal insulation of cavity walls (with masonry or concrete inner and outer leaves) by filling with urea-formaldehyde (UF) foam systems.*
Amendment slip
1: AMD 6262.

BS 5628: *Code of practice for use of masonry:*
Part 3: 1985 *Materials and components, design and workmanship.*

BS 6232: *Thermal insulation of cavity walls by filling with blown man-made mineral fibre:*
Part 1: 1982 *Specification for the performance of installation systems.*
Amendment slip
1: AMD 5428
Part 2: 1982 *Code of practice for installation of blown man-made mineral fibre in cavity walls with masonry and/or concrete leaves.*

BS 6915: 1988 *Specification for design and construction of fully supported lead sheet roof and wall coverings.*

BS 8200: 1985 *Code of practice for design of non-loadbearing external vertical enclosures of buildings.*

BS 8102: 1990 *Code of practice for protection of structures against water from the ground.*

BS 8208: *Guide to assessment of suitability of external cavity walls for filling with thermal insulants:*
Part 1: 1985 *Existing traditional cavity construction.*

BS 8215: 1991 *Code of practice for design and installation of damp-proof courses in masonry construction.*

BS 8298: *Code of practice for design and installation of natural stone cladding and lining.*

CP 102: 1973 *Code of practice for protection of buildings against water from the ground,*
Amendment slips
1: AMD 1151,
2: AMD 2196,
3: AMD 2470.

CP 143 *Code of practice for sheet roof and wall coverings:*
Part 1: 1958 *Aluminium, corrugated and troughed*
Part 5: 1964 *Zinc*
Part 10: 1973 *Galvanised corrugated steel*
Part 12: 1970 *Copper*
Amendment slips
1: AMD 863,
2: AMD 5193
Part 15: 1973 (1986) *Aluminium*
Amendment slip
1: AMD 4473,
Part 16: 1974 *Semi-rigid asbestos bitumen sheet.*

CP 297: 1972 *Precast concrete cladding (non-loadbearing).*

DD 93: 1984 *Methods for assessing exposure to wind-driven rain.*

## Approved documents published by the Department of the Environment and the Welsh Office as at October 1991

The following Approved Documents have been revised in conjunction with the Building Regulations 1991 and will take effect on 1 June 1992

**A** Structure
**B** Fire safety
**C** Site preparation and resistance to moisture
**E** Resistance to the passage of sound
**G** Hygiene
**K** Stairs, ramps and guards
**M** Access and facilities for disabled people
**N** Glazing - materials and protection
**Reg 7** Materials and workmanship

The following Approved Documents, originally approved for the purposes of the Building Regulations 1985, have not been revised, and will continue to be approved for the purposes of the Building Regulations 1991 with effect from 1 June 1992:

**D** Toxic substances, 1985 edition
**F** Ventilation, 1990 edition
**H** Drainage and waste disposal, 1990 edition
**J** Heat producing appliances, 1990 edition
**L** Conservation of fuel and power, 1990 edition

Note that the Manual to the Building Regulations 1985 has been withdrawn.

Printed in the United Kingdom for HMSO
Dd 302349 C50 3/94 9091